CAKES
AND
BAKING

Photography by Peter Barry
Designed by Claire Leighton and
 Helen Johnson
Edited by Jillian Stewart and Kate Cranshaw

3566
© 1994 Coombe Books
This edition published 1994
for Parragon Book Service Ltd., Unit 13-17, Avonbridge Trading Estate,
Atlantic Road, Avonmouth, Bristol BS11 9QD
All rights reserved.
Printed in Hong Kong
ISBN 1-85813-578-8

CAKES
AND
BAKING

PARRAGON

Contents

Introduction

There is something of great social significance about baking, whether it is a cake or a delicious dessert. Preparing a sweet treat is always an indication of goodwill, of wanting to share, and of wanting to be sociable. Cakes in particular tend to to be baked often for special occasions, but cakes are not just for birthdays, although there is a great trend nowadays to ice a cake into all sorts of appropriate designs: fairytales for children's birthday parties or a golfing range for Dad's fiftieth. These are fine, and particularly magnificent to look at, but often the energy and ingenuity spent on the icing is inversely proportional to the attention given to the cake mixture. Such cakes can be too good to cut, but not so good to eat! The recipes here are about delicious ingredients and wholesome and mouthwatering tastes.

Cake making techniques and methods vary tremendously and, indeed, are also of social significance. A cake mixture can be rushed, literally in a minute or two, from food processor bowl into the oven. Modern pressures of work and family commitments, all to be squeezed into a day that is never long enough, are such that a cake is frequently thrown together in this way and the result, happily, is great. The food processor's greatest use is probably for cake making. It is hard, however, not to feel nostalgic for those childhood days when mum, perched on the kitchen stool, would work away at the cake with that comforting rhythmic ringing of the wooden spoon beating butter and sugar against the stoneware mixing bowl, followed by the gentle folding in of the flour. Of course there are still plenty of people who make cakes in the traditional fashion and their cakes taste great too. It's all a matter of personal preference, and how much time you have on your hands. It is nice though to think that a handmade cake, as opposed to a machine-made cake, has a little extra love and sympathy stirred into it.

Cakes and baked desserts are an international phenomenon. Every country has its own specialities, and usually a wide variety of types. In Britain, among many others, we have our classic Victoria sponge. In Germany they have a wonderful Christmas stollen bread. In Ireland they have cakes made with Guinness. In America there are cheesecakes and buckwheat puddings and in France there are delicate pastries and gateaux. In this book there are recipes for many of these specialities, among many more diverse and delectable baked goodies with which to wickedly laden your table.

ALMOND LAYER CAKE

Definitely not for the diet conscious, but delicious for those wishing to sin. This wonderful creamy gateau is ideal for serving with tea, or even as a dessert.

SERVES 8

60g/2oz dried white breadcrumbs
120ml/4 fl oz milk
2 tbsps rum
90g/3oz unsalted butter
90g/3oz caster sugar
6 eggs, separated
90g/3oz roasted almonds, ground
570ml/1 pint double cream
2 tbsps icing sugar
60g/2oz roasted almonds, finely chopped
Whole blanched almonds, lightly toasted,
     for decoration

---

1. Put the breadcrumbs into a large bowl and pour over the milk and half the rum. Allow to stand for 15 minutes or until the liquid has been completely absorbed.

2. Put the butter in a large bowl and beat until soft. Gradually add the sugar and continue mixing until it is light and fluffy.

3. Beat in the egg yolks, one at a time, mixing well to prevent it curdling. Fold in the soaked breadcrumbs to blend evenly.

4. Whisk the egg whites until they are stiff, but not dry. Fold these into the egg and butter mixture, along with the ground almonds.

5. Line and lightly grease 3 × 20cm/8-inch round cake tins, and dust each one lightly with a little flour.

6. Divide the cake mixture equally between the three tins. Bake in an oven preheated to 180°C/350°F/Gas Mark 4, for 30-35 minutes, or until well risen and golden brown.

7. Allow the cakes to cool briefly in the tins before gently loosening the sides and turning onto a wire rack to cool completely.

8. Whip the cream until it is stiff, then beat in the icing sugar and remaining rum.

9. Reserve one third of the cream and fold the finely chopped almonds into the rest.

10. Sandwich the cake layers together with the almond cream, then spread a thin layer of the plain cream onto the top, using the rest for piping rosettes of cream onto the top of the cake. Decorate with the toasted whole almonds and serve.

TIME: Preparation takes 40 minutes, cooking takes 35 minutes.

COOK'S TIP: Refrigerate the cream for at least 2 hours before whippping, to obtain better results.

TO FREEZE: The almond cakes can be frozen for up to 1 month, but should be filled and decorated just before serving or they will become too soggy.

KUGELHOPF

This Continental yeasted cake is ideal for serving at tea-time.

SERVES 8

520g/1lb 2oz plain flour
225ml/8 fl oz warm milk
4 tsps yeast
2 tbsps plum liqueur, e.g. Slivovitz or
    Mirabelle Eau de Vie
90g/3oz raisins
¼ tsp salt
Scant 120g/4oz sugar
2 eggs
175g/6oz butter, softened
35g/5 tbsps slivered almonds

---

1. Mix together 75g/2½oz flour with half the warm milk and all the yeast and leave for 1 hour in a warm place.

2. Pour the liqueur over the raisins and leave to marinate.

3. Sift the remaining flour into a mixing bowl with the salt and sugar. Make a well in the centre and add the eggs together with the remaining milk. Gradually incorporate the flour and mix well to form a sticky dough.

4. Knead the dough in the bowl for at least 5 minutes.

5. Knead the softened butter and the yeast mixture into the dough until well mixed.

6. Set the dough aside in a warm place for one hour, or until it has risen and tripled in volume.

7. When the dough has tripled in size, mix in the raisins and almonds.

8. Grease a kugelhopf or brioche mould with melted butter. Place the dough evenly in the mould.

9. Bake in an oven preheated to 180°C/350°F/Gas Mark 4, for 45 minutes. Allow to rest in the tin for 15 minutes before turning out.

TIME: Preparation takes about 40 minutes, plus 2 hours rising time, and cooking takes about 45 minutes.

VARIATION: The almonds could be replaced with walnuts, and the weight of the raisins increased slightly to compensate.

COOK'S TIP: The more you knead the dough the lighter and fluffier your kugelhopf will be.

DEVIL'S FOOD CAKE

This classic American cake is very rich, so serve in small slices.

SERVES 10-12

120g/4oz plain chocolate, broken into
    squares
225ml/8 fl oz milk
120g/4oz caster sugar
120g/4oz butter
3 eggs, separated
¼ tsp vanilla essence
225g/8oz plain flour
2 tsps baking powder

Frosting
90g/3oz icing sugar
30g/1oz cocoa powder
45g/1½oz butter
2 tbsps water
60g/2oz caster sugar

1. Place the chocolate, half the milk and all the sugar in a bowl over a pan of boiling water and cook, stirring, until the chocolate has melted and the mixture is scalding hot.

2. Beat the butter until soft, then beat in the egg yolks one at a time. Add the vanilla essence to the remaining milk, and sift the flour and baking powder together.

3. Add the flour and vanilla milk mixtures alternately to the butter mixture, beating well after each addition to obtain a smooth batter. Stir in the chocolate mixture.

4. Beat the egg whites until stiff, then fold them gently into the cake batter. Pour this into a greased cake tin, and bake in an oven preheated to 180°C/350°F/Gas Mark 4, for about 35 minutes, or until a skewer inserted in the centre comes out clean. Turn out onto a rack to cool.

5. For the frosting, sift the icing sugar and cocoa into a bowl. Put the butter with the water and caster sugar over a low heat in a heavy-based saucepan. When the sugar has dissolved and the butter melted, bring to the boil and quickly pour into the centre of the dry ingredients.

6. Beat with a wooden spoon to make a smooth icing, then gently stir the icing until thick enough to coat the back of a spoon. Continue to stir the icing occasionally, until thick enough to leave a trail.

7. Spread the frosting over the top and sides of the cake and decorate by roughing-up the icing with the tip of a table knife.

TIME: Preparation takes about 45 minutes and cooking takes about 40 minutes.

SERVING IDEA: Serve with cream, ice-cream or crème fraîche.

ANGEL FOOD CAKE

This American cake is made with lots of egg whites and no fat, so it has a very light texture and is almost white in colour.

SERVES 6-8

Cake
90g/3oz plain flour
30g/1oz cornflour
Pinch of salt
175g/6oz caster sugar
11 egg whites
1 tsp cream of tartar
1 tsp vanilla essence

Frosting
460g/1lb sugar
120ml/4 fl oz cold water
2 egg whites

Raspberries and mint leaves, to decorate

1. Sieve the flour, three times, together with the cornflour, salt and half the sugar.

2. Whisk the egg whites in a large, clean bowl until just foaming, then add the cream of tartar. Whisk until the mixture is stiff but not dry, whisking in the remaining sugar 1 tbsp at a time. Beat in the vanilla essence. The mixture should be glossy and hold its peaks.

3. Sieve ⅓ of the flour mixture over the egg whites and gently, but quickly, fold it in using a metal tablespoon. Fold in the remaining flour in two batches.

4. Immediately turn the mixture into an ungreased angel food cake tin and bake in an oven preheated to 180°C/350°F/Gas Mark 4, for 40-50 minutes or until the top springs back when lightly touched.

5. Turn the tin upside down on its legs. If the tin doesn't have legs, place upside down over the neck of a bottle. Leave until completely cold. The cake should slide easily out of the tin.

6. To make the frosting, dissolve the sugar in the water in a heavy-based saucepan then boil, without stirring, until the syrup reaches the hard-ball stage, 120°C/248°F on a sugar thermometer. Beat the egg whites until stiff, then gradually beat in the hot sugar syrup.

7. Continue beating until the frosting is cool then spread immediately over the cake, forming peaks and swirls in the frosting with a palette knife. Decorate with some raspberries and mint leaves.

TIME: Preparation takes about 45 minutes, and cooking takes 40-50 minutes for the cake and about 15-20 minutes for the syrup.

WATCHPOINT: Do not overbeat the egg whites for the cake, they should not be dry. Do not grease the cake tin.

COOK'S TIP: Angel food cake tins are available in specialist kitchen shops.

COOK'S TIP: Follow the recipe instructions very carefully to achieve the best results.

CHRISTMAS CAKE

This rich, moist fruit cake is made without sugar or eggs and is suitable for vegans.

MAKES 1 × 23cm/9 inch square cake

120ml/4 fl oz clear honey
175ml/6 fl oz safflower or sunflower oil
90g/3oz soya flour
280ml/½ pint water
1 tbsp rum or 1 tsp rum essence
Grated rind and juice of 1 orange
Grated rind and juice of 1 lemon
60g/2oz flaked almonds
90g/3oz dried figs, chopped
90g/3oz dried dates, chopped
60g/2oz dried apricots, chopped
225g/8oz wholewheat self-raising flour
Pinch salt
2 tsps mixed spice
225g/8oz currants
225g/8oz sultanas
225g/8oz raisins

---

1. Cream the honey and the oil together.

2. Mix the soya flour with the water and gradually add to the oil and honey mixture, beating well.

3. Beat in the rum and the grated rind and juice of the orange and lemon. Add the almonds, figs, dates and apricots.

4. Mix the wholewheat flour with the salt and spice and mix together the currants, sultanas and raisins.

5. Stir half the flour and half the currant mixture into the soya cream, then stir in the remainder. Spoon into a greased and lined 23cm/9-inch square cake tin.

6. Cover with two or three layers of brown paper and bake in an oven preheated to 160°C/325°F/Gas Mark 3 for 3¼-3½ hours, or until a skewer inserted into the centre comes out clean.

7. Cool for 10 minutes in the tin, then turn out onto a wire rack to cool. Store in an airtight tin.

TIME: Preparation takes about 40 minutes, cooking takes 3¼-3½ hours.

COOK'S TIP: This cake will keep well but is best made three to four weeks before cutting. Store, wrapped in foil or greaseproof paper, in an airtight tin.

SERVING IDEAS: Leave plain or decorate with glazed fruits. Try serving the Yorkshire way with chunks of cheese.

VARIATION: Other dried fruits may be used instead of figs, dates and apricots but make sure that the overall measurements stay the same.

HAZELNUT TORTE

Hazelnuts add a lovely flavour to this German gateau.

SERVES 8

5 eggs, separated
175g/6oz sugar
90ml/6 tbsps water
200g/7oz plain flour
1 tsp baking powder
175g/6oz ground, skinned hazelnuts
1 tsp vanilla essence
2 tbsps icing sugar
225ml/8 fl oz double cream, whipped
Fresh strawberries, for decoration

1. Beat the egg yolks and sugar with an electric hand mixer for about 5 minutes or until thick and pale. Slowly beat in the water.

2. Sift the flour and baking powder together. Mix with 120g/4oz of the nuts. Gently fold the flour mixture into the egg yolks using a metal tablespoon.

3. Beat the egg whites until soft peaks form. Gently fold the beaten whites into the batter. Pour into a greased and floured 25cm/10-inch springform cake tin.

4. Bake in an oven preheated to 190°C/375°F/Gas Mark 5, for 30 minutes or until light and springy to the touch.

5. Cool the cake on a rack. When completely cooled, split the cake into 2 layers.

6. Fold the vanilla, icing sugar, and remaining nuts into the whipped cream. Spread some of the cream between the cake layers, and sandwich together.

7. Use the remaining cream to decorate the top of the cake and chill until serving time. Decorate with fresh strawberries, if wished. Chill until serving time.

TIME: Preparation takes 35-45 minutes, and cooking takes about 30 minutes. Chill before serving.

COOK'S TIP: To remove skins of the hazelnuts they should be baked in an oven at 180°C/350°F/Gas Mark 4, for 7-12 minutes or until golden. Shake the tray occasionally. Wrap the nuts in a tea-towel and rub them to remove the skins.

COCONUT LAYER CAKE

The addition of fresh coconut keeps this cake nice and moist.

SERVES 8

225g/8oz butter
460g/1lb sugar
3 eggs, separated
340g/12oz flour
2 tsps baking powder
225ml/8 fl oz coconut milk
150g/5oz freshly grated coconut
Seedless raspberry jam

1. Cream together the butter and sugar until soft and light, then beat in the egg yolks one by one.

2. Sift together the flour and the baking powder and add to the butter mixture alternately with the coconut milk, stirring gently after each addition until the batter is smooth.

3. Stir in 90g/3oz of the grated coconut. Whisk the egg whites until stiff and fold them gently into the cake batter.

4. Divide the batter between 3 greased cake tins and bake in an oven preheated to 180°C/350°F/Gas Mark 4, for about 25 minutes, or until springy to the touch. Turn out onto a wire rack to cool.

5. To assemble the cake, sandwich the layers together with raspberry jam. Spread another layer of raspberry jam over the top of the cake and cover with the remaining coconut.

TIME: Preparation takes about 30 minutes and cooking takes about 25 minutes.

COOK'S TIP: When grating the coconut, don't include the brown skin. The liquid inside a fresh coconut is coconut water. Coconut milk can be bought in cans from many large supermarkets.

IRISH COFFEE CAKE

This delicious tipsy coffee cake is soaked with whisky and topped with cream.

SERVES 6-8

Ingredients
120g/4oz butter or margarine
120g/4oz caster sugar
2 eggs
120g/4oz plain flour
1 tsp baking powder
2 tsps instant coffee dissolved in 2 tbsps hot
    water

Syrup
120g/4oz sugar
140ml/¼ pint strong coffee
3 tbsps Irish whiskey

Topping
140ml/¼ pint whipping cream
1 heaped tsp icing sugar
1 tbsp Irish whiskey
Whole hazelnuts

1. In a bowl, cream together the butter and sugar until light and fluffy, then beat in the eggs one at a time, mixing well.

2. Sift the flour and baking powder together and fold ⅔ of it into the mixture using a metal tablespoon. Add the coffee mixture, and blend well.

3. Fold in the remainder of the flour. Pour the mixture into a greased and floured 20cm/8-inch ring tin and bake in an oven preheated to 180°C/350°F/Gas Mark 4, for 35-40 minutes or until a skewer inserted into the centre of the cake comes out clean. Turn out onto a wire rack to cool.

4. To make the syrup, heat the sugar in the coffee until dissolved, then boil rapidly for 1 minute. Remove from the heat and blend in the whiskey. Return the cooled cake to the well-washed tin and pour the syrup over it. Let it soak for several hours.

5. For the topping, beat the cream with the icing sugar and whiskey.

6. Turn the cake out onto a serving plate and decorate with the cream and whole hazelnuts. Chill before serving.

TIME: Preparation takes about 30 minutes, plus 2-3 hours soaking time. Cooking takes 35-40 minutes. Chill cake before serving.

VARIATION: Add a little grated orange rind to the topping mixture for a contrast of flavours.

BEE STING CAKE

This recipe is a favourite in cake shops all over Germany.

SERVES 8

Cake
175g/6oz self-raising flour
Salt
150g/5oz butter or margarine
90g/3oz sugar
2 eggs
½ tsp vanilla essence
1-2 tbsps milk

Topping
60g/2oz sugar
60g/2oz butter
1 tbsp milk
60g/2oz flaked almonds

Filling
60g/2oz sugar
2 tbsps cornflour
3 egg yolks
140ml/¼ pint milk
¼ tsp vanilla or almond essence
90ml/3 fl oz double cream, whipped

1. Sift the flour and pinch of salt into a large mixing bowl.

2. Cream the butter until soft and gradually add the sugar, beating until the mixture is pale and fluffy. Beat in the eggs one at a time and add the vanilla.

3. Using a metal spoon, fold in the milk and the flour, alternating between the two. Use enough milk to bring mixture to thick dropping consistency. Grease and flour a springform cake tin and spoon in the cake mixture.

4. Heat the topping ingredients in a saucepan to just dissolve the sugar. Sprinkle the top of the cake mixture lightly with flour and pour on the topping. Bake in an oven preheated to 190°C/375°F/Gas Mark 5, for 25-30 minutes. The topping will caramelise slightly as the cake bakes.

5. Meanwhile, prepare the filling. Combine the sugar, cornflour and egg yolks in a bowl and whisk until light. Gently pour on the milk and gradually whisk into the egg yolk mixture. Strain the mixture into a heavy-based saucepan and cook over very gentle heat until the mixture coats the back of a spoon.

6. Add the vanilla or almond essence and allow to cool, placing clingfilm directly over the top of the custard as it cools. When the custard is completely cool, fold in the cream.

7. To assemble the cake, remove it from the tin and cut in half, horizontally through the middle. Sandwich the cake together with the filling and chill thoroughly before serving.

TIME: Preparation takes 40 minutes. Cooking takes 40 minutes.

WATCHPOINT: Do not allow the topping to become too hot. Heat just long enough to dissolve the sugar.

FLOURLESS CHOCOLATE CAKE

This is part mousse, part soufflé, part cake and completely heavenly! It's light but rich, and adored by chocolate lovers everywhere.

SERVES 6

460g/1lb plain chocolate
2 tbsps strong coffee
2 tbsps brandy
90g/6 tbsps sugar
6 eggs
280ml/½ pint whipping cream
Icing sugar
Fresh whole strawberries, to decorate

1. Melt the chocolate in the top of a double boiler. Stir in the coffee and brandy and leave to cool slightly.

2. Using an electric mixer, gradually beat the sugar into the eggs until the mixture is thick and mousse-like. When the beaters are lifted the mixture should mound slightly.

3. Whip the cream until soft peaks form. Beat the chocolate until smooth and shiny, and gradually add the egg mixture to it.

4. Fold in the cream and pour the cake mixture into a well greased 22cm/9-inch deep cake tin lined with a disk of greaseproof paper in the bottom.

5. Stand the tin in a bain marie, and bake in an oven preheated to 180°C/350°F/Gas Mark 5 for about 1 hour and then turn off the oven, leaving the cake inside to stand for 15 minutes.

6. Loosen the sides of the cake carefully from the tin and allow the cake to cool completely before turning it out.

7. Invert the cake onto a serving plate and carefully peel off the paper. Place strips of greaseproof paper on top of the cake, leaving even spaces in between the strips.

8. Sprinkle the top with icing sugar and carefully lift off the paper strips to form a striped or chequerboard decoration. Decorate with whole strawberries.

PREPARATION: To make a bain marie, use a roasting tin and fill with enough warm water to come halfway up the sides of the cake tin.

WATCHPOINT: Do not allow the water around the cake to boil at any time. If it starts to bubble, pour in some cold water to reduce the temperature.

COOK'S TIP: If wished, the cake may be prepared a day in advance and can be left well-covered overnight. This will produce a denser texture.

SPICE CAKE

Serve this well flavoured cake with cream or crème fraîche.

225g/8oz butter
460g/1lb sugar
4 eggs
340g/12oz plain flour
2 tsps baking powder
½ tsp powdered cloves
1 tsp cinnamon
1 tsp allspice
225ml/8 fl oz buttermilk
150g/5oz raisins

1. Cream the butter with the sugar until soft and light, then beat in the eggs one at a time.

2. Sift the flour together with the baking powder and spices. Add this alternately to the butter mixture with the buttermilk, stirring well after each addition to obtain a smooth batter. Fold in the raisins.

3. Pour the batter into a greased cake tin and bake in an oven preheated to 180°C/350°F/Gas Mark 4, for about 50 minutes or until a skewer inserted in the centre comes out clean. Turn the cake out onto a rack and leave to cool.

TIME: Preparation takes about 20 minutes and cooking takes 50 minutes.

VARIATION: If buttermilk is unavailable, use natural yogurt instead.

CINNAMON BUTTERCREAM CAKE

*A cake that doesn't need baking is convenient any time, and perfect for summer.
It's very rich, though, so it will go a long way.*

SERVES 10-12

275g/10oz sugar
90ml/6 tbsps water
1 cinnamon stick
8 egg yolks
460g/1lb unsalted butter, softened
24 sponge fingers
90ml/6 tbsps brandy
90g/3oz toasted almonds, roughly chopped
90g/3oz plain chocolate, coarsely grated

1. Combine the sugar, water and cinnamon stick in a small, heavy-based saucepan and bring to the boil, stirring until the sugar dissolves.

2. Allow to boil briskly, without stirring, until the syrup reaches a temperature of 115°C/235°F on a sugar thermometer, or until a small amount dropped into cold water forms a soft ball.

3. While the sugar syrup is boiling, beat the egg yolks in a large bowl with an electric hand mixer until they are thick and pale lemon coloured. Soften the butter by beating until light and fluffy.

4. When the syrup is ready, quickly pour it in a thin, steady stream into the egg yolks, beating constantly with the electric mixer.

5. Continue beating for about 10-15 minutes, or until the mixture is thick, smooth and creamy. Allow to cool to room temperature.

6. Beat in the softened butter, a spoonful at a time. Chill the mixture until it is of spreading consistency.

7. Cut the sponge fingers to fit closely together in a 20cm/8-inch square cake tin. Line the tin with lightly greased foil or greaseproof paper.

8. Lightly spread some of the buttercream on one side of half the biscuits and place them, icing side down, in the tin. Use small pieces of biscuit to fill in any corners, if necessary.

9. Sprinkle over half of the brandy, soaking each biscuit well. Spread over another layer of buttercream and place on the remaining biscuits, pushing them down to stick them into the cream. Sprinkle over the remaining brandy and cover the top with buttercream, reserving some for the sides. Place the cake in the refrigerator and chill until firm.

10. When the icing is firm, remove the cake from the refrigerator and lift it out of the tin using the foil or paper. Slide the cake off the paper onto a flat surface and spread the sides with the remaining buttercream. Press the chopped almonds into the sides and decorate the top with grated chocolate. Transfer to a serving dish and serve immediately.

TIME: Preparation takes about 45 minutes, with about 3 hours in the refrigerator to set the buttercream.

31

BARM BRACK

This Irish speciality bread contains lots of dried fruit – serve it thinly sliced with butter.

MAKES 2 loaves

½ tsp salt
½ tsp cinnamon
Pinch grated nutmeg
460g/1lb plain flour
1 sachet active dry yeast
75g/2½oz caster sugar
60g/2oz softened butter
1 egg
225ml/8 fl oz lukewarm milk
225g/8oz sultanas
90g/3oz currants
90g/3oz chopped, mixed peel

1. Add the salt and spices to the flour and sift into a large mixing bowl. Stir in the yeast and sugar, and rub in the butter.

2. Lightly beat the egg and add the milk. Make a well in the centre of flour, add the liquid and beat very well by hand, or in a mixer fitted with a dough hook, until the batter becomes stiff and elastic.

3. Fold in the sultanas, currants and mixed peel and cover the bowl with lightly greased cling film. Leave the bowl in a warm place for 1-2 hours, to allow the dough to rise.

4. Divide the mixture between two greased 20.5 × 11.5cm/8½ × 4½ inch loaf tins. Cover again and allow to rise for 30 minutes.

5. Bake in the centre of an oven preheated to 190°C/375°F/Gas Mark 5, for about 1 hour, or until a skewer inserted into the centre of the loaf comes out clean.

6. Dissolve 1 tbsp of sugar in 60ml/4 tbsps of hot water and brush over the brack, return it to the oven for 5 minutes with the heat turned off. Turn out onto a rack to cool.

TIME: Preparation takes about 20 minutes plus 1½-2½ hours rising time. Cooking takes about 1 hour.

VARIATION: The mixture may be baked in two 18cm/7-inch cake tins if preferred.

POUND CAKE

A plain cake that complements fruit salads to perfection, and is also a welcome addition to the afternoon tea table.

SERVES 8

340g/12oz softened butter
340g/12oz caster sugar
¼ tsp vanilla essence
5 eggs
1 tbsp orange flower water
2 tsps baking powder
340g/12oz plain flour, sieved

1. Cream together the butter, sugar and vanilla until pale and fluffy.

2. Beat in the eggs one at a time, together with the orange flower water and the baking powder. Fold in the flour in thirds, using a metal tablespoon to obtain a thick batter.

3. Spoon the batter into either a non-stick or a greased and lined loaf tin and bake in an oven preheated to 180°C/350°F/Gas Mark 4, for about 45 minutes, or until a skewer inserted into the centre of the cake comes out clean.

4. Turn out onto a cake rack to cool.

TIME: Preparation takes 15 minutes and cooking takes about 45 minutes.

VARIATION: Chopped hazelnuts or walnuts may be added to the cake batter.

PRALINE SPONGE CAKE

This extravagant cake is well worth its slightly time-consuming assembly and will earn you many compliments.

SERVES 4

Sponge cake

4 eggs

150g/5oz sugar

150g/5oz plain flour, sieved

30g/1oz butter, melted

Praline cream filling

1 tbsp powdered gelatine

75g/5 tbsps sugar

3 egg yolks

4 tsps flour

460ml/16 fl oz milk

5 tbsps praline, see below

175ml/6 fl oz cream

2 tbsps crushed praline

Whipped cream and crushed praline, to
    decorate

1. In a bowl, beat the eggs with the sugar using an electric handwhisk. Place over a pan of simmering water and beat the mixture until it increases in volume and thickens. Remove the bowl from the heat and continue to beat until the mixture has cooled and forms ribbons when dropped from a spoon.

2. Gently fold in first the flour and then the melted butter using a metal tablespoon. Fill a greased and floured cake tin three quarters full and bake in an oven preheated to 160°C/325°F/Gas Mark 3, for about 25 minutes, or until springy to the touch. Turn out onto a wire rack to cool, then slice horizontally into four layers.

3. Meanwhile, to make the filling, sprinkle the gelatine over 3-4 tbsps cold water and leave for 5 minutes to soften and swell.

4. Mix together the sugar, egg yolks and flour. Bring the milk to a boil with the praline, stirring to dissolve the latter, then pour it over the egg yolk mixture and mix together well. Return the mixture to the saucepan and stir over a low heat without boiling until thickened. Set aside.

5. Melt the gelatine over hot water until all the crystals have dissolved. Stir the gelatine into the warm cream filling, then allow this to cool for 10-15 minutes, stirring occasionally.

6. Whip the cream until stiff, then fold it gently but thoroughly into the filling together with the crushed praline.

7. Place one sponge layer on a plate, spread a quarter of the filling over, then top with another sponge layer. Continue in this way, finishing with the final quarter of cream filling. Using a spatula to give a smooth finish, spread the cream over the top and sides of the cake.

8. Chill the cake for 2 hours. Before serving, decorate with a little whipped cream and crushed praline.

TIME: Preparation takes about 45 minutes and cooking takes 35 minutes.

PREPARATION: To make praline, caramelize equal quantities of whole almonds and caster sugar. Turn out onto a greased baking tray to cool, then break up and grind in a food processor.

Black Forest Cake

SERVES 8-10

Pastry layer

½ quantity pastry recipe for Cherry Cake

1 tbsp redcurrant jelly, melted

Cake

150g/5oz unsalted butter

6 eggs

1 tsp vanilla essence

225g/8oz sugar

60g/2oz plain flour

60g/2oz cocoa powder

Syrup

60g/4 tbsps caster sugar

3 tbsps water

2 tbsps kirsh

Filling and topping

850ml/1½ pints double cream

60g/2oz icing sugar

60ml/4 tbsps kirsch

225g/8oz canned, pitted cherries, drained

225g/8oz plain chocolate, grated

Fresh cherries, to decorate

1. Make the pastry according to the recipe for Cherry Cake. Lightly grease a baking sheet and pat the pastry out into a round about 5mm/¼ inch thick. Prick lightly with a fork and bake in a preheated oven at 190°C/375°F/Gas Mark 5 for 15 minutes or until browned lightly around the edge and firm in the centre. Cut out a 17.5cm/7 inch circle while it is still warm. Allow to cool completely on the baking sheet after loosening it.

2. Soften the butter then cream it with a hand beater or electric mixer. Beat the eggs, vanilla and sugar together on high speed until thick and fluffy. Sift in the flour and cocoa 2 tbsps at a time, folding it in with a metal spoon. Fold in the butter.

3. Divide the mixture between 3 x 17.5cm/7-inch lined, greased and floured cake tins and bake for 10-15 minutes, or until a knife inserted in the middle of the cakes comes out clean. Allow to cool in the tins for about 5 minutes then loosen and turn out onto wire racks.

4. Bring the sugar and water, for the syrup, to the boil in a pan, stirring until the sugar dissolves. Raise the heat and boil rapidly for 5 minutes. Cool, then stir in the kirsch. Place a tray under the cooling racks and prick the cake layers with a fork. Pour the syrup over and leave to soak.

5. Beat the cream until it thickens slightly, add the sugar and beat until it forms peaks that hold their shape. Fold in the kirsch.

6. Place the pastry on a plate and brush with the redcurrant jelly. Place one cake layer on top and press down lightly. Spread a third of the cream over and cover with half the cherries. Repeat the layering. Press down the top layer and cover the top and sides with a thin layer of cream. Press grated chocolate around the sides of the cake to cover. Decorate the top with piped rosettes of cream, the remaining chocolate and fresh cherries.

STOLLEN

This makes an attractive centre-piece on the tea table, particularly around Christmas time.

MAKES 1 Loaf

250g/9oz strong white flour
Pinch of salt
15g/½oz fresh yeast
15g/½oz light muscovado sugar
100ml/3½ fl oz milk, warmed
1 egg, beaten

Filling
1 egg
150g/5oz ground almonds
60g/2oz black poppy seeds, plus extra for
  decoration
60g/2oz raisins, soaked overnight
60g/2oz currants
60g/2oz cherries, chopped
60g/2oz light muscovado sugar, finely
  ground
30g/1oz dates, chopped
Juice ½ lemon
Almond essence

60g/2oz butter
1 egg, beaten to glaze

1. Place the flour and salt in a bowl.

2. Cream the yeast and sugar together, add the milk and stir well.

3. Add the beaten egg and leave for a few minutes in a warm place.

4. Add the mixture to the flour and mix in to form a dough. Knead well for 5 minutes.

5. Put into a clean bowl, cover with a damp cloth and leave to prove in a warm place for 40 minutes or until doubled in size.

6. To make the filling, beat the egg, reserving a little, and add all the other filling ingredients. Mix well – the mixture should be fairly moist.

7. To assemble, knock back the dough and roll out to a rectangle 30.5 × 20cm/12 × 8 inches.

8. Working with the short sides in front of you, dot 30g/1oz of the butter over two thirds of the dough from the top. Fold over from the bottom to one third up, then fold from top to bottom. Seal the edges and make one quarter turn.

9. Roll out to a rectangle shape again and repeat with the remainder of the butter. Fold over as before but do not roll out.

10. Place in the refrigerator for about 30 minutes. Remove and roll out a rectangle as before.

11. Cover with the filling, leaving a tiny margin around the edges. Roll up from a short side to make a fat sausage shape and tuck in the ends. Brush with beaten egg.

12. Mark out in 2.5cm/1-inch slices by snipping either side with scissors.

13. Cover with the remaining poppy seeds and leave to prove for a further 15 minutes.

14. Bake in an oven preheated to 200°C/400°F/Gas Mark 6 for 30 minutes or until risen and golden.

TIME: Preparation takes 25 minutes, cooking takes 30 minutes. Proving takes 1 hour 40 minutes.

Rich Fruit Cake with Guinness

A deliciously moist fruit cake which is easy to make.

SERVES 12-16

225g/8oz soft margarine
225g/8oz dark brown sugar
4 medium eggs
275g/10oz wholemeal flour
2 tsps mixed spice
500g/1lb 2oz mixed dried fruit
140ml/¼ pint Guinness

1. Cream the margarine and sugar together until light and fluffy.

2. Beat in the eggs one at a time, beating well between each addition.

3. Gradually stir in the flour and mixed spice, then mix in the dried fruit.

4. Add 60ml/4 tbsps of the Guinness to the mixture and stir in gently until evenly blended.

5. Spoon the mixture into a deep 17.5cm/7 inch loose-bottomed cake tin and make a deep well in the centre, this allows the finished cake to have a flat top.

6. Cook for 1 hour at 160°C/325°F/Gas Mark 3 and then turn down to 150°C/300°F/Gas Mark 2 for a further 1½ hours or until a skewer inserted into the centre of the cake comes out clean.

7. Allow the cake to cool in the tin.

8. Remove the cake from the tin and turn upside down. Prick the base of the cake all over with a skewer and slowly pour over the remaining Guinness.

9. Store in a cool place for at least a week before eating. Cover with greaseproof paper.

TIME: Preparation takes about 15 minutes, cooking takes 2½ hours.

SERVING IDEAS: Use for birthdays and special occasions or serve with chunks of tasty cheese.

VARIATION: This mixture can be cooked in two 460g/1lb loaf tins, reduce the final cooking time and cook until a skewer inserted into the cake comes out clean.

APPLE CAKE

This apple cake is based on a German recipe, and tastes equally delicious whether served alone with coffee or with custard as a dessert.

SERVES 6

2 large apples
120g/4oz plain flour
120g/4oz caster sugar
2 tsps baking powder
Pinch salt
2 eggs
120g/4oz melted butter

1. Peel, core and dice the apples.

2. Sift together the flour, sugar, baking powder and salt and beat in the eggs.

3. Beat in the melted butter, then stir in the diced apple.

4. Butter a cake tin well, pour in the cake batter and bake in an oven preheated to 180°C/350°F/Gas Mark 4, for about 35 minutes.

TIME: Preparation takes about 15 minutes and cooking takes about 35 minutes.

COOK'S TIP: Sprinkle the cake with a little cinnamon just before baking.

SERVING IDEAS: Accompany the cake with a cinnamon-flavoured custard sauce.

CHOCOLATE MARBLE CAKE

This attractive cake is the ideal accompaniment to a fresh fruit salad, but is also popular served on its own with coffee.

SERVES 8

340g/12oz butter, softened
400g/14oz sugar
6 eggs
2 tsps baking powder
400g/14oz plain flour
2 tbsps cocoa powder
120ml/4 fl oz milk
½ tsp vanilla essence

1. Cream the butter and the sugar together until very light and fluffy. Beat in the eggs one at a time, mixing well. Sift the baking powder with the flour, and fold into the mixture to obtain a smooth, thick cake batter.

2. Transfer one third of the batter to a clean bowl. Dissolve the cocoa powder in the milk, stir it into the batter and set aside.

3. Add the vanilla essence to the remaining cake batter.

4. Thickly butter an oblong cake tin. Fill the bottom with half the plain cake batter. Pour in the chocolate cake batter and then top with the remaining plain batter. Swirl a knife through all the layers to create a marbled effect.

5. Bake in an oven preheated to 180°C/350°F/Gas Mark 4, for 45-50 minutes, or until a skewer inserted into the centre of the cake comes out clean. When cooked, turn the cake out onto a wire rack and allow to cool.

TIME: Preparation takes about 25 minutes and cooking takes 45-50 minutes.

COOK'S TIP: The plain cake batter can be flavoured with a few drops of orange flower water instead of the vanilla essence.

VARIATION: Melted chocolate can be used in place of the cocoa for a stronger flavour.

LEMON CAKE

Using lemon zest and juice in this cake gives it a subtle tang.

SERVES 6-8

120g/4oz butter
225g/8oz sugar
1 lemon
2 eggs, separated
225g/8oz flour
1½ tsps baking powder
120ml/4 fl oz milk

1. Cream together the butter and sugar until soft and light. Beat in the grated rind of the lemon and 2 tsps of the juice, followed by the egg yolks.

2. Sift together the flour and the baking powder and add to the butter mixture alternately with the milk, beating well after each addition to obtain a smooth batter.

3. Whisk the egg whites until stiff and fold them gently into the cake batter using a metal tablespoon.

4. Turn the batter into a greased cake tin and bake in an oven preheated to 180°C/350°F/Gas Mark 4, for 45 minutes, or until springy to the touch. Turn out onto a cake rack and leave to cool.

TIME: Preparation takes 15 minutes and cooking takes about 45 minutes.

SERVING IDEA: Split the cake in half and sandwich together with lemon curd. Dust the top with icing sugar.

SOUR CREAM CAKE

An extremely moreish cake from across the Atlantic. More or less cinnamon can be added as preferred.

SERVES 8

120g/4oz butter
200g/7oz sugar
2 eggs
150ml/5 fl oz carton soured cream
1 tsp bicarbonate of soda
175g/6oz plain flour
1½ tsp baking powder
1 tsp vanilla essence

Topping
60g/2oz demerara sugar
2 tbsps chopped mixed nuts
2 tsps cinnamon

1. In a large bowl, cream together the butter and sugar until light and fluffy. Beat in the eggs, one at a time, and beat in the soured cream mixed with the bicarbonate of soda.

2. Sieve together the flour and baking powder and fold in gently using a metal tablespoon. Add the vanilla.

3. Mix topping ingredients together. Pour half the cake mixture into a greased 23cm/9-inch cake tin and sprinkle with half the topping.

4. Pour in the remaining cake mixture and sprinkle with the rest of the topping.

5. Bake in an oven preheated to 180°C/350°F/Gas Mark 4, for 40 minutes or until risen and a skewer inserted into the centre of the cake comes out clean.

TIME: Preparation takes about 20 minutes and cooking takes 40 minutes.

SERVING IDEA: Serve warm for afternoon tea or with coffee.

LEMON TART

A classic dessert, loved by all age groups.

SERVES 6-8

120g/4oz butter
225g/8oz wholemeal flour
60g/2oz brown sugar
2 egg yolks
A little water

Filling

4 eggs, separated
120g/4oz brown sugar
60g/2oz ground almonds
120g/4oz unsalted butter, softened
140ml/¼ pint double cream, lightly
    whipped
Grated rind and juice of 2 lemons

---

1. Rub the butter into the flour until the mixture resembles fine breadcrumbs.

2. Mix in the sugar, and add the egg yolks and a little water to mix to make a dough.

3. Roll out to line a fairly deep loose-bottomed flan tin.

4. Prick the bottom, cover with a sheet of greaseproof paper and fill with baking beans, rice or pasta. Bake blind in an oven pre-heated to 220°C/425°F/Gas Mark 7, for about 10 minutes. Remove the beans and paper.

5. Meanwhile, prepare the filling. Mix the egg yolks with the sugar and add the ground almonds, butter, whipped cream and lemon juice, beating until smooth and creamy.

6. Whisk the egg whites until the peaks hold their shape, then fold into the yolk mixture with the lemon rind using a metal tablespoon.

7. Pour into the pastry case and bake at a reduced temperature of 180°C/350°F/Gas Mark 4, for 40 minutes, or until slightly risen and golden brown. Leave to cool in the tin.

TIME: Preparation takes 25 minutes, cooking takes 50 minutes.

SERVING IDEA: Serve decorated with piped whipped cream.

WATCHPOINT: Do not overbeat the filling as it is liable to overflow during cooking.

PLUM AND HONEY COBBLER

*A cobbler is a traditional pie, so called because the scones which decorate the top
are reminiscent of the cobbles found on old roads.*

SERVES 6

900g/2lbs ripe plums, halved and stoned
60-120ml/4-6 tbsps clear honey
225g/8oz wholemeal self-raising flour
2 tbsps caster sugar
60g/2oz butter or margarine
75-120ml/5-6 tbsps milk
1 egg, beaten

1. Put the plums into an ovenproof dish along with the honey. Cover with a sheet of foil and cook in a preheated oven at 200°C/400°F/Gas Mark 6, for 20 minutes.

2. After this time the plums should be soft and a certain amount of juice should have formed in the dish. Remove from the oven and cool completely.

3. Put the flour and the sugar into a large bowl and using your fingers, rub in the butter until the mixture resembles fine breadcrumbs.

4. Using a round bladed knife, stir in the milk and egg, so that the mixture forms a soft dough.

5. Turn the dough out onto a lightly floured work surface and knead it until it is smooth.

6. Roll the dough out until it is about 1.25cm/½-inch thick.

7. Cut the dough into rounds using a 5cm/2-inch plain cutter to form the cobbles.

8. Carefully arrange the scone cobbles in an overlapped circle around the top edge of the dish of plums, overlapping each scone slightly.

9. Brush the top of each scone with a little milk and sprinkle with a little extra sugar. Return the plum cobbler to the oven and cook for about 25 minutes or until the scones are firm, risen and well browned.

TIME: Preparation takes 30 minutes, cooking takes about 45 minutes.

VARIATION: Use any variation of fresh fruit in place of the plums.

SERVING IDEA: This dessert is delicious served hot with vanilla ice cream.

SHOO-FLY PIE

This classic American pie is made with molasses and has a crumble topping. Its name is said to originate from the fact that flies are attracted to the pie because it is very sweet.

SERVES 6

Pastry
120g/4oz plain flour
Pinch salt
75g/2½oz solid vegetable fat
15g/½oz butter
Milk

Crumb mixture
90g/3oz plain flour
½ tsp cinnamon
Pinch nutmeg, ground cloves and ginger
Pinch of salt
120g/4oz brown sugar
30g/1oz butter

Filling
1½ tsps bicarbonate of soda
175ml/6 fl oz boiling water
175g/6oz molasses
1 egg yolk, beaten well

1. To prepare the pie crust, sieve the flour and salt into a mixing bowl and rub in the vegetable fat and butter until the mixture resembles breadcrumbs.

2. Mix in enough milk to form a firm dough. Chill for about 10 minutes, then roll out and use to line a 20cm/8-inch pie plate.

3. To make the crumb mixture, combine flour with the spices, salt and sugar. Rub in the butter until the mixture forms coarse crumbs.

4. To make the filling, dissolve the bicarbonate of soda in the boiling water and blend in the molasses and egg yolk thoroughly.

5. Fill the pie with alternating layers of the crumb and filling mixture, ending with crumbs.

6. Bake in an oven preheated to 200°C/ 400°F/Gas Mark 6, for about 15 minutes or until the crust edges start to brown. Lower the temperature to 180°C/350°F/Gas Mark 4, and bake for about 20 minutes, or until the filling is set.

TIME: Preparation takes about 30 minutes and cooking takes 30-40 minutes.

SERVING IDEAS: Serve warm or cold with whipped cream or vanilla ice cream.

WALNUT AND HAZELNUT TART

A variation on the well-known Bakewell Tart, this pie is filling and is best served after a light main course.

SERVES 6

225g/8oz shortcrust pastry
3 eggs, separated
175g/6oz sugar
40g/4 tbsps ground hazelnuts
40g/4 tbsps ground walnuts
3 tbsps raspberry jam

1. Roll out the pastry and use to line a 23cm/9-inch buttered flan ring, pressing the pastry well into the base and sides.

2. Run a rolling pin over the edge of the pan to remove the excess. Set aside to rest in a cool place.

3. Beat together the egg yolks and the sugar until light in colour. Add the ground nuts and mix thoroughly.

4. Whisk the egg whites until stiff, and gently fold into the egg yolk mixture.

5. Spread the jam over the pastry and then pour in the nut mixture.

6. Bake in an oven preheated to 180°C/350°F/Gas Mark 4, for about 35 minutes. Allow to cool a little before serving. This tart can also be served cold.

TIME: Preparation takes about 35 minutes and cooking also takes about 35 minutes.

VARIATION: A single type of nut – hazelnut, walnut or almond – could be used.

BLUEBERRY PIE

Blueberries are available frozen from many large supermarkets, but use fresh ones if you can.

SERVES 8

Double quantity pastry for Pumpkin Pie recipe

Filling
460g/1lb blueberries
2 tbsps cornflour
60ml/4 tbsps water
2 tbsps lemon juice
225g/8oz sugar
1 egg, beaten with a pinch of salt

1. Prepare the pastry in the same way as for the Pumpkin Pie recipe.

2. Divide the pastry in half and roll out one half to form the base. Use it to line a loose-bottomed flan ring. Chill the pastry in the tin and the remaining half of the pastry while preparing the filling.

3. Place the blueberries in a bowl and blend the cornflour with the water and lemon juice. Pour it over the fruit, add the sugar and mix together gently.

4. Spoon the fruit filling into the pastry base. Roll out the remaining pastry on a lightly-floured surface and cut it into strips.

5. Use the strips to make a lattice pattern on top of the filling and press the edges to stick them to the pastry base. Cut off any excess pastry.

6. Brush the pastry edge and the lattice strips lightly with the beaten egg and bake in an oven preheated to 220°C/425°F/Gas Mark 7, for about 10 minutes.

7. Reduce the heat to 180°C/350°F/Gas Mark 4 and bake for a further 40-45 minutes. Serve warm or cold.

TIME: Preparation takes about 30-40 minutes and cooking takes about 50-55 minutes.

COOK'S TIP: Taste the blueberries before deciding how much sugar to add – it may not be necessary to add the full amount. If using frozen berries, drain them very well first.

VARIATION: Other fruits such as raspberries, blackberries or blackcurrants may be used in the pie instead of blueberries.

CHERRY TART

This tart contains fresh cherries in a custard filling, and is quite irresistible.

SERVES 6-8

Pastry

175g/6oz self-raising flour

3 tbsps sugar

Salt

150g/5oz butter

2 egg yolks

Dash vanilla essence or 1 tsp grated lemon
    rind

1-2 tbsps milk or water

Filling

570g/1¼lbs fresh cherries

1 slice white or wholemeal bread, made
    into crumbs

120g/4oz sugar

Cinnamon or nutmeg

60g/2oz toasted hazelnuts, chopped

2 egg yolks

90ml/3 fl oz single cream

1. To make the pastry, sift the flour, sugar and salt into a large bowl. Rub in the butter until the mixture resembles fine breadcrumbs.

2. Make a well in the centre and add the egg yolks, vanilla or lemon rind and 1 tbsp of the milk or water.

3. Mix these into the flour using a fork, adding the extra liquid if necessary. Knead together quickly until smooth. If the mixture is too soft chill briefly.

4. Press into a loose-bottomed flan tin to line the base and sides, then chill for 15 minutes.

5. To prepare the filling, wash the cherries and stone them using a cherry pitter or a vegetable peeler. Alternatively, cut them in half to remove the stones easily.

6. Sprinkle the top of the pastry with the breadcrumbs and then spread the cherries over evenly. Sprinkle with sugar and a pinch of cinnamon or nutmeg if wished, then scatter over the hazelnuts.

7. Beat the egg yolks and cream together and pour over the top. Bake in a preheated oven at 200°C/400°F/Gas Mark 6, for 20-30 minutes or until the pastry is pale brown and the filling has risen and set. Serve warm or cold cut into wedges.

TIME: Preparation takes about 30 minutes, cooking takes about 20-30 minutes.

VARIATION: Other berries may be used instead of cherries. Apples, pears, plums or apricots can also be used. If using canned fruit, be sure to drain well.

COOK'S TIP: This tart does not keep well, so serve on the day it is made.

PUMPKIN PIE

Try this as a special autumn treat when pumpkins are plentiful.

SERVES 8-10

Pastry
120g/4oz plain flour
Pinch salt
60g/2oz butter, margarine or lard
Cold milk

Pumpkin filling
460g/1lb cooked and mashed pumpkin
2 eggs
280ml/½ pint evaporated milk
120g/4oz brown sugar
1 tsp ground cinnamon
¼ tsp ground allspice
Pinch nutmeg

Pecan halves, for decoration

1. To prepare the pastry, sift the flour and a pinch of salt into a mixing bowl. Rub in the fat until the mixture resembles fine breadcrumbs.

2. Stir in enough cold milk to bring the mixture together into a firm ball. Cover and chill for about 30 minutes before use.

3. Roll out the pastry on a lightly-floured surface to a circle about 28cm/11 inches in diameter, and use to line a 25cm/10-inch round pie dish. Prick the surface lightly with a fork.

4. Combine all the filling ingredients in a mixing bowl and beat with an electric mixer until smooth. Alternatively, use a food processor.

5. Pour the filling into the pie crust and bake in an oven preheated to 220°C/425°F/ Gas Mark 7, for 10 minutes.

6. Lower the temperature to 180°C/350°F/ Gas Mark 4 and bake for a further 40-50 minutes, or until the filling is set. Decorate with a circle of pecan halves.

TIME: Preparation takes about 30 minutes and cooking takes about 50-60 minutes.

COOK'S TIP: Pricking the base of the pastry lightly before filling it will prevent it from rising up in an air bubble in the middle of the pie.

SERVING IDEA: Serve warm or cold with whipped cream.

KOUIGN AMAN

This rich pastry is traditionally sliced and served warm with coffee.

SERVES 4

340g/12oz plain flour
1½ tbsps fresh yeast
225ml/8 fl oz warm water
175g/6oz butter, at room temperature
120g/4oz sugar
Flour for dredging

1. Place the flour in a mound on a work surface or in a bowl. Crumble in the fresh yeast and add the water little by little, working with your fingers to form the ingredients into a dough.

2. When all the ingredients have been worked together, knead the dough for a few minutes, then form it into a ball, and set it aside to rise in a warm place, in a large greased plastic bag, for about 1½ hours.

3. When the dough has risen, roll it out into a square, leaving a slight mound in the centre.

4. Place the butter in the centre, flattening it down slightly. Place the sugar on the butter and fold in each of the four sides to cover it.

5. Roll the dough out on a well-floured surface to form a long rectangle. Fold one end into the centre and fold the other end in over the first.

6. Give the dough a quarter turn and then roll and fold the dough again. Place the dough in the refrigerator for 10 minutes.

7. After the dough has rested, roll and fold the dough a third time.

8. Form the dough into a round and place on a non-stick baking sheet. Bake in an oven preheated to 200°C/400°F/Gas Mark 6 for about 40 minutes.

9. Leave the cooked Kouign Aman to rest slightly and serve while still warm.

TIME: Preparation takes about 40 minutes, plus a total of 2 hours 10 minutes resting time, and cooking takes about 40 minutes.

COOK'S TIP: Kouign Aman is prepared in the same way as puff pastry, except that only three turns are necessary.

WATCHPOINT: On the third turn the butter tends to 'sweat'; keep the work surface well floured and cook the finished dough immediately.

ECLAIRS

Think of French pastry and eclairs immediately spring to mind.

MAKES 12

Choux pastry
200ml/7 fl oz water
90g/3oz butter
90g/3oz plain flour, sifted
3 eggs, beaten

Crème patissière
1 whole egg, separated
1 egg yolk
60g/2oz sugar
1 tbsp cornflour
1½ tbsps flour
280ml/½ pint milk
Few drops vanilla essence

Glacé icing
460g/1lb icing sugar
Hot water
Few drops vanilla essence

1. Put the water and butter for the pastry in a saucepan and bring to a rapid boil. Take off the heat, stir in the flour all at once and beat just until the mixture leaves the sides of the pan.

2. When cool, gradually add the egg. Beat well in between each addition until smooth and shiny, it should be of soft dropping consistency, but holding its shape well. You may not need to add all the egg.

3. Fill a piping bag fitted with a plain nozzle with the mixture and pipe out 12 strips about 7.5cm/3 inches long, spaced well apart on lightly-greased baking sheets.

4. Sprinkle the sheets lightly with water and place in an oven preheated to 180°C/350°F/Gas Mark 4. Immediately increase oven temperature to 190°C/375°F/Gas Mark 5, and bake for 20-30 minutes or until the pastry is very crisp.

5. To prepare the Crème Patissière, mix the egg yolks and sugar together, sift in the flours and add about half the milk, stirring well. Bring the rest to the boil and pour onto the yolk mixture, stirring constantly.

6. Return to the pan and stir over heat until boiling point is reached. Take off the heat. Whip the egg white until stiff but not dry then fold into the mixture and return to the heat.

7. Cook gently for about 1 minute, stirring occasionally. Add the vanilla essence. Pour the mixture into a bowl and press greaseproof paper directly onto the surface and leave to cool.

8. Sift the icing sugar into a bowl and add hot water, stirring constantly until the mixture covers the back of a wooden spoon but runs off slowly. Add the vanilla essence.

9. To assemble, cut the choux pastry almost in half lengthways and pipe or spoon in the Crème Patissière. Using a large spoon, coat the top of each eclair with a layer of icing. Allow to set before serving.

TIME: Preparation takes 40 minutes, cooking takes 30-40 minutes.
COOK'S TIP: Water sprinkled on the baking sheet helps the pastry rise.

ROYAL MAZUREK

Mazureks are flat Polish pastry cakes and there are many different recipes for these. Although the dough needs careful handling, the result is well worth the effort.

SERVES 8

175g/6oz butter or margarine
60g/4 tbsps sugar
90g/6 tbsps blanched almonds, finely chopped
½ tsp grated lemon rind
275g/10oz plain flour
Yolks of 2 hard-boiled eggs, sieved
1 raw egg yolk
Pinch salt
Pinch cinnamon
1 egg, beaten with a pinch salt
Apricot jam and raspberry or cherry jam
Icing sugar

1. Cream the butter and the sugar together until light and fluffy. Stir in the almonds, lemon rind, flour and sieved egg yolks by hand.

2. Add the raw egg yolk and a pinch of salt and cinnamon, and mix all the ingredients into a smooth dough. This may be done in a food processor. Wrap and chill for about 1 hour.

3. Roll out ⅔ of the dough to a rectangle about 5mm/¼-inch thick and place on a baking sheet. If the dough cracks, press back into place. Keep the remaining ⅓ of the dough in the refrigerator.

4. Roll out the remaining dough and cut into thin strips, again about 5mm/¼-inch thick. Arrange these strips on top of the dough in a lattice pattern and press the edges to seal.

5. Brush the pastry with the beaten egg. Bake in an oven preheated to 190°C/375°F/Gas Mark 5, for about 20-30 minutes, or until light golden brown and crisp. Loosen the pastry from the baking sheet but do not remove until completely cool.

6. Place the pastry on a serving plate and spoon some of the jam into each of the open spaces of the lattice work, alternating the two flavours. Dust lightly with icing sugar before serving.

TIME: Preparation takes about 30 minutes, plus 1 hour chilling for the pastry. Cooking takes about 20-30 minutes.

VARIATION: Use other finely chopped nuts in the pastry and other varieties of jam.

COOK'S TIP: If the lattice strips break, press the ends together and they will stick together again.

GALETTE DES ROIS

This pastry, which translates as "kings' cake", is traditionally served in France at Epiphany, when a charm is baked into it and the finder is entitled to be king or queen of the festivities.

SERVES 4

60g/2oz softened butter

60g/2oz sugar

1 egg

60g/2oz ground almonds

2 tbsps pastry cream

1 tsp rum

460g/1lb puff pastry

1 egg, beaten

1. Cream together the butter and sugar, adding the egg and ground almonds to obtain a thick cream.

2. Mix in the pastry cream and the rum until thoroughly combined.

3. Roll out the pastry thinly and cut into eight circles of which half should be slightly larger than the rest.

4. Place the four smaller circles on a greased baking sheet. Prick them all over with a fork. Place the almond cream in a piping bag and pipe over the centre of the circles, leaving a wide edge all the way round.

5. Brush a little beaten egg around the edges of the pastry circles.

6. Cover them with the larger circles, pressing the edges together well then crimping them to seal the galettes completely.

7. Brush the tops with the remaining beaten egg and bake in an oven preheated to 220°C/425°F/Gas Mark 7, for about 20 minutes, until the galettes are golden brown.

TIME: Preparation takes about 30 minutes and cooking takes approximately 25 minutes.

SERVING IDEA: Accompany with a custard sauce.

PREPARATION: For method for pastry cream see Malakoff Aunt Ida recipe.

PARIS-BREST

This enticing confection is a traditional French pastry that will enhance any dinner party. A few chopped strawberries, in season, could be added to the cream filling for a delicious variation.

SERVES 4

Choux pastry

120ml/4 fl oz water
55g/1¾oz butter
¼ tsp salt
75g/2½oz plain flour, sieved
2-2½ eggs
1 egg, beaten
1 tbsp slivered almonds
Icing sugar

Filling

225ml/8 fl oz double cream
60g/4 tbsps crushed praline

1. Place the water, butter and salt in a saucepan and bring to the boil. When the butter has melted and the water is boiling, add the flour all at once. Beat continuously for a few minutes until the dough comes away cleanly from the sides of the pan and forms a ball.

2. Remove the pan from the heat and beat in the eggs one by one, mixing in well, to obtain a smooth glossy paste.

3. Place the pastry in a piping bag fitted with a plain nozzle, and pipe out 10cm/ 4-inch rings onto a greased baking sheet. Brush the tops with beaten egg and sprinkle with the almonds. Bake for 20 minutes in an oven preheated to 200°C/400°F/Gas Mark 6, or until golden brown firm and risen. Remove the choux rings from the oven, allow them to cool and then slice them in half horizontally.

4. To make the filling, whip the cream until stiff then fold in the praline. Place the filling in a piping bag fitted with a plain nozzle.

5. Pipe the filling into the bottom halves of the choux rings, then replace the tops. Sift icing sugar over the pastries and serve immediately.

TIME: Preparation takes about 35 minutes and cooking takes about 20 minutes.

WATCHPOINT: It is important that the choux rings are properly cooked before being removed from the oven, or they will fall apart.

COOK'S TIP: When you add the first egg to the choux pastry, this will separate, but continue beating and it will become smooth again.

BUYING TIP: Praline is an almond brittle which is available from speciality food shops. For home preparation see Praline Sponge Cake: PREPARATION.

FRESH PEACH AND HAZELNUT MERINGUE

This gateau makes an impressive dessert for a dinner party.

SERVES 6-8

3 large egg whites
175g/6oz caster sugar
90g/3oz ground hazelnuts
280ml/½ pint double cream
4 large firm ripe peaches
Few whole roasted hazelnuts

1. Whisk the egg whites until stiff and then add the sugar, a tablespoon at a time, still whisking until glossy and stiff. Using a metal spoon, gently fold in the ground hazelnuts.

2. Divide the mixture between two greased and lined 18cm/7-inch sandwich tins, levelling it out.

3. Bake in the centre of an oven preheated to 180°C/350°F/Gas Mark 4, for 20-30 minutes. Allow the tins to cool before turning the meringues out onto a wire rack. Take off the base papers.

4. Whip the cream and to half of it add the chopped flesh of two of the peaches. Use this mixture to sandwich the meringues together. Decorate the top with the rest of the cream, the remaining peaches (carefully sliced), and the whole hazelnuts.

TIME: Preparation takes about 30 minutes and cooking takes 20-30 minutes.

VARIATION: Use other fruit such as raspberries, bananas, strawberries or a mixture of exotic fruits.

CRÈME BRÛLÉE WITH ALMONDS

Flavouring this classic dessert with almonds adds to its delicious richness.

SERVES 4

3 eggs
420ml/¾ pint double cream
2 tbsps caster sugar
2-3 drops almond essence, or more to taste
4 tsps ground almonds
3-4 tbsps sugar

1. Beat the eggs with the cream and the 2 tbsps sugar.

2. Add the almond essence and mix in well.

3. Add the ground almonds, stir in well and pour into a shallow ovenproof dish.

4. Place the dish in a roasting tin filled with enough warm water to come halfway up the sides of the dish.

5. Bake in an oven preheated to 150°C/300°F/Gas Mark 2 for about 40 minutes.

6. Allow to cool and then put in the refrigerator to chill for at least 4 hours.

7. Just before serving sprinkle the remaining sugar over the chilled custard in a thin, even layer.

8. Caramelize under a hot grill, watching the dish carefully and turning it if need be so the sugar browns evenly.

TIME: Preparation takes about 15 minutes, plus at least 4 hours chilling time, and cooking takes about 40 minutes.

VARIATION: Different flavoured custards can be obtained by replacing the almond extract either with a liqueur or with vanilla essence.

BAKED APPLES IN OVERCOATS

Pastry sweetened with cinnamon and spices combines with a rich fruit filling to make this warming winter dessert.

SERVES 6

340g/12oz plain flour
¼ tsp salt
¼ tsp cinnamon
¼ tsp ground nutmeg
175g/6oz butter
75-105ml/5-7 tbsps iced water
6 medium dessert apples
6 prunes, pitted
6 dried apricots
2 tbsps raisins
1 egg, beaten to glaze
Fresh mint, to decorate
Fresh cream, to serve

---

1. Sift the flour, salt and spices into a large bowl. Cut the butter into dice and rub into the flour until the mixture resembles fine breadcrumbs.

2. Mix in enough water to produce a smooth pliable dough. Divide the dough into six pieces and roll each out into a 20cm/8-inch square.

3. Peel the apples with a sharp knife and carefully remove the centre cores with an apple corer. Chop the prunes and the apricots and mix these with the raisins.

4. Place one prepared apple in the centre of each pastry square, and fill the cavities with equal amounts of the dried fruit mixture.

5. Brush the edges of each square with a little water, and draw them up and around the sides of the apples, sealing them well with a little water and trimming off any excess pastry to give a neat finish.

6. Roll out the pastry trimmings, cut into decorative leaves and stick the leaves onto each apple for decoration.

7. Glaze each pastry apple with the beaten egg and place on a lightly greased baking sheet.

8. Bake the apples in an oven preheated to 180°C/350°F/Gas Mark 4, for 20-25 minutes or until golden brown.

9. Decorate with sprigs of mint and serve hot with fresh cream or custard.

TIME: Preparation takes about 30 minutes, cooking time takes 20-25 minutes.

COOK'S TIP: For an extra rich pastry, use 1 egg yolk and half the amount of water in this recipe.

VARIATION: Use pears instead of apples in this recipe.

TO FREEZE: These apples freeze well after baking and should be thawed, then re-heated, before eating.

CARAMEL CUSTARD WITH ORANGE AND CORIANDER

This is one of the best loved desserts in Spain. Fragrant coriander gives it new appeal and its flavour is marvellous with orange.

SERVES 8

175g/6oz sugar
90ml/6 tbsps water
3 small oranges
850ml/1½ pints milk
1 tbsp coriander seeds, crushed
6 eggs
2 egg yolks
175g/6oz sugar

1. To prepare the caramel, put the sugar and water in a heavy-based saucepan. Heat, stirring to dissolve the sugar.

2. Once the sugar is dissolved, bring to the boil over high heat and cook, without stirring, to a golden brown, watching the colour carefully.

3. While the caramel is cooking, heat 8 ramekin dishes. When the caramel is brown, pour an equal amount into each and swirl quickly to coat the base and sides. Leave to cool and harden in the dishes.

4. Grate the rind from the oranges and scald with the milk and coriander in a saucepan. Set aside to infuse.

5. Beat the eggs, yolks and the sugar together until light and fluffy. Gradually strain on the milk, stirring well in between each addition. Gently strain the mixture over the caramel in each dish.

6. Place the dishes in a bain-marie and bake in an oven preheated to 170°C/325°F/Gas Mark 3, for about 40 minutes, or until a knife inserted into the centre of the custards comes out clean. Lower the oven temperature slightly if the water begins to boil around the dishes.

7. Chill the custards for at least 3 hours or overnight until completely cold and set.

8. To serve, loosen the custards from the the dishes with a small knife and turn out onto individual plates. Cut off all the pith from around the oranges and segment the flesh. Place some orange around each custard and serve immediately.

TIME: Preparation takes about 30-40 minutes, cooking time for the custards is about 40 minutes.

PREPARATION: To make a bain-marie, pour enough warm water into a roasting tin, to come half way up the sides of the ramekins. Do not let the water boil.

HOT APPLE PIZZA

A delicious dessert – perfect with yogurt or cream.

SERVES 4-6

15g/½oz fresh yeast
60ml/2 fl oz lukewarm water
90g/3oz strong wholemeal flour
60g/2oz strong white flour
½ tsp ground cinnamon
15g/½oz butter or margarine
½ tbsp concentrated apple juice

Topping
2 red skinned dessert apples
30g/1oz raisins
30g/1oz hazelnuts
1 tbsp concentrated apple juice
15g/½oz butter or margarine

---

1. Cream the yeast with the water, add 1 teaspoon of the flour and leave in a warm place for 10-15 minutes until frothy.

2. Mix together the flours and cinnamon, and rub in the butter.

3. Add the yeast mixture and concentrated apple juice to the flour.

4. Mix to a stiff dough, adding more warm water if necessary. Knead well.

5. Roll the dough out to a circle, about 20-23cm/8-9 inches in diameter. Cover with oiled cling film and leave to rise for 10-15 minutes in a warm place.

6. To prepare the topping, slice the apples evenly and arrange over the base.

7. Sprinkle the raisins, hazelnuts and concentrated apple juice over the apples and dot with the butter or margarine.

8. Bake on the middle shelf of an oven preheated to 200°C/400°F/Gas Mark 6, for 15-20 minutes.

TIME: Preparation takes, including rising, 45 minutes. Cooking takes 15-20 minutes.

VARIATION: Use other fruits, except oranges in place of the apples.

PEACHY CHEESECAKE

A fairly rich cheesecake with a smooth texture.

SERVES 6

Base

12 digestive biscuits, crushed or processed
    into fine crumbs
45g/1½oz melted butter or margarine

Topping

400g/14oz curd cheese
420ml/¾ pint soured cream or Greek
    yogurt
2 tbsps clear honey
1½ tsps vanilla essence or lemon juice
2 eggs, beaten
1½ tbsps wholewheat self-raising flour
Sliced peaches, to decorate

1. Combine the biscuit crumbs and melted butter then press the mixture into the bottom of a greased, loose-bottomed 23cm/9-inch flan tin or dish.

2. Combine the curd cheese with 200ml/ 7 fl oz of the soured cream or yogurt, 1 tbsp honey, ¾ tsp vanilla essence, the eggs and all the flour.

3. Pour the mixture onto the biscuit base and bake in an oven preheated to 150°C/300°F/Gas Mark 2, for about 20 minutes or until just set.

4. Remove from the oven and increase the oven temperature to 230°C/450°F/Gas Mark 8.

5. Combine the remaining soured cream or yogurt with the rest of the honey and vanilla essence and spread over the top of the cake. Smooth over with a palette knife or spatula.

6. Return to the oven and bake for 5 minutes. Allow to cool before decorating with sliced peaches. Chill thoroughly before serving.

TIME: Preparation takes 25 minutes, cooking takes 25 minutes.

VARIATION: For special occasions decorate with seasonal fruit such as strawberries or raspberries and chocolate curls.

COOK'S TIP: Use canned fruit in natural juice if fresh is not available.

BAKED RASPBERRY APPLES

A lovely combination which is perfectly complemented by cream or yogurt.

SERVES 6

---

2 tbsps concentrated apple juice
60ml/4 tbsps water
2 tbsps honey
1 tsp mixed spice
3 very large eating apples
225g/8oz raspberries

---

1. Put the concentrated apple juice, water, honey and mixed spice into a large bowl and mix together well.

2. Wash the apples and, with a sharp knife, make deep zig-zag cuts around the middle of each apple.

3. Take one half of the apple in each hand and twist gently until the two halves come apart.

4. Remove the cores and immerse each apple in the apple juice mixture.

5. Place the apples in an ovenproof dish and bake in an oven preheated to 200°C/400°F/Gas Mark 6, for 20-25 minutes or until just soft.

6. Remove from the oven and top with the raspberries.

7. Pour the remaining apple juice mixture over the raspberries and return to the oven at the reduced temperature of 150°C/300°F/Gas Mark 2, for 10 minutes. Serve at once.

TIME: Preparation takes 10 minutes, cooking takes 30-35 minutes.

SERVING IDEAS: Serve topped with a spoonful of Greek yogurt or whipped cream.

COOK'S TIP: Frozen raspberries may be used instead but make sure they are well thawed out.

CRUNCHY CHOCOLATE MERINGUE

A mouthwatering dessert. The chopped hazelnuts give the meringue a crunchy texture.

SERVES 10

Meringue
6 egg whites
340g/12oz caster sugar
120g/4oz finely chopped hazelnuts

Chocolate sauce
275g/10oz plain chocolate
340ml/12 fl oz double cream

1. In a large bowl, whisk the egg whites until stiff then gradually beat in the sugar until the mixture is glossy. Fold in the chopped hazelnuts using a metal tablespoon, saving a few for decoration.

2. Divide the mixture between 3 x 20cm/ 8-inch sandwich tins lined with bakewell paper. Bake in an oven preheated to 180°C/350°F/Gas Mark 4, for 30-35 minutes, or until the meringue is crisp on top.

3. After baking, leave the meringues in the tins for one minute, then turn out carefully and peel away the paper. The meringue should be crispy on top and soft underneath.

4. To make the sauce, break the chocolate into squares and reserve a couple for decoration. Place the chocolate in a bowl and add 175ml/6 fl oz of the cream. Place over a pan of simmering water and heat gently until the chocolate has melted completely, then leave until cold.

5. Whip the remaining cream. Place one meringue on a plate, spread half of the chocolate sauce over it and smother the sauce with half the whipped cream. Cover with the second meringue and repeat with the remaining sauce and cream. Place last meringue on top and decorate with the reserved nuts and chocolate, grated.

TIME: Preparation takes about 40 minutes and cooking takes 30-35 minutes.

COOK'S TIP: To ensure the meringue layers cook at the same rate, move the tins around during baking if you have a gas oven.

POACHED PEACHES

*Fresh peaches with Amarena cherries are poached in white wine for a light,
summer dessert.*

SERVES 4

6 ripe peaches
1 can Amarena cherries (reserve the juice)
120ml/4 fl oz white wine
2 tbsps ground almonds

1. Cut the peaches in half and remove the stones.

2. Place a few cherries in the hollow of each peach half, then place them side by side in a small baking tin or cake tin. Add a spoonful of the reserved cherry juice to the centre of each peach.

3. Pour the wine into the bottom of the tin and sprinkle the ground almonds over the peaches.

4. Bake in an oven preheated to 180°C/ 350°F/Gas Mark 4, for about 25 minutes, checking the level of the wine from time to time. Serve either hot or chilled with whipped cream, mascarpone or crème fraîche.

TIME: Preparation takes about 10 minutes and cooking takes approximately 25 minutes.

VARIATION: Nectarines may be substituted for the peaches if preferred.

COOK'S TIP: The almonds should be golden brown after cooking, if necessary, place under a hot grill for 1 minute.

MALAKOFF AUNT IDA

This simple nursery-style pudding is easy to digest after a rich meal.

SERVES 4-6

Pastry cream
4 egg yolks
3½ tbsps sugar
½ tsp vanilla essence
30g/1oz cornflour
225ml/8 fl oz milk

120g/4oz sugar
3 tbsps water
4 egg whites
Cocoa powder, to decorate

1. Mix together the egg yolks, the 3½ tbsps sugar, the vanilla essence and cornflour.

2. Bring the milk to the boil and stir it into the above mixture. Pour the pastry cream back into the saucepan, replace on a gentle heat and stir continuously until thick.

3. Pour the pastry cream into a heatproof glass serving dish and allow to cool.

4. Caramelize the 120g/4oz sugar and the water. When lightly coloured carefully pour in 75ml/5 tbsps of water. Reheat to dissolve the caramel, which will now remain liquid.

5. Pour half the caramel over the pastry cream and spread evenly.

6. Beat the egg whites until foamy. Gradually pour in the remaining caramel, beating continuously to obtain a stiff meringue mixture.

7. Pipe the meringue onto the caramel-topped pastry cream. Sift over a little cocoa and serve immediately, otherwise the egg whites will fall.

TIME: Preparation and cooking take a total of about 40 minutes.

COOK'S TIP: To caramelize the sugar, heat with the water in a small heavy-based pan. Stir to dissolve the sugar then boil over a high heat, without stirring, until the liquid turns a pale caramel colour.

CREAMY RICE PUDDING

Rice pudding makes a good warming dessert on a cold winters day.

SERVES 4

200g/7oz short or medium-grain rice
Nutmeg
120g/4oz sugar
Pinch of salt
910ml/1 pint 12 fl oz scalded milk

---

1. Wash and drain the rice well. Put it into a greased baking dish and grate over a little nutmeg to taste.

2. Sprinkle over the sugar and the salt, then pour in the scalded milk. Do not stir.

3. Bake the pudding in an oven preheated to 180°C/350°F/Gas Mark 4, for about 1½ hours, without stirring, until the rice grains are separate and show above the milk, which should be thick and creamy.

TIME: Preparation takes 10 minutes and cooking takes 1½ hours.

SERVING IDEAS: Serve with a fruit sauce such as apple or raspberry.

BUCKWHEAT AND RAISIN PUDDING

Of all the cereals or 'kashas' used in Polish cooking, buckwheat is the most highly prized.

SERVES 6-8

850ml/1½ pints milk
1 vanilla pod
90g/3oz butter or margarine
225g/8oz buckwheat
4 eggs, separated
175g/6oz sugar
Grated rind of ½ lemon
120-175g/4-6oz raisins
Red cherry jam and cream, to serve

1. Boil the milk with the vanilla pod in a large saucepan, and stir in 60g/2oz of the butter until melted.

2. Pick over the buckwheat and add it to the milk, stirring well. Cook, uncovered, over a low heat, stirring occasionally to prevent it from sticking.

3. When the mixture thickens, transfer it to an ovenproof dish with a tight fitting lid. Bake in an oven preheated to 190°C/375°F/Gas Mark 5, for 45 minutes. Remove the vanilla pod and allow the mixture to cool slightly.

4. Beat the egg yolks with the sugar until light and fluffy. Add lemon rind, mix with the buckwheat, and stir in the raisins.

5. Whisk egg whites until stiff peaks form and fold into the buckwheat mixture.

6. Smooth the top of the pudding and dot with the remaining butter. Return to the oven and bake for a further 30 minutes.

7. Serve topped with cherry jam and cream, if wished.

TIME: Preparation takes about 20 minutes, cooking takes a total of 1 hour 25 minutes.

VARIATION: Substitute sultanas, currants or mixed peel for the raisins if preferred. Use a cinnamon stick in place of the vanilla pod.

COOK'S TIP: Vanilla pods and cinnamon sticks may be used several times. Rinse and dry after use and store in an air tight container.

APPLE AND CRANBERRY CRUMBLE

Serve this delicious crumble hot with natural yogurt or serve cold with ice cream.

SERVES 4

680g/1½lbs Bramley or other cooking
   apples
60g/2oz raw cane sugar
175g/6oz fresh or frozen and defrosted
   cranberries

Crumble
90g/3oz butter or margarine
60g/2oz sunflower seeds
90g/3oz raw cane or demerara sugar
150g/5oz wholewheat flour
120g/4oz porridge oats

1. Peel, core and dice the apples. Place in a saucepan with the sugar and about 2 tbsps water. Cook gently until just beginning to soften.

2. Add the cranberries and cook for a further minute. Remove from the heat.

3. Melt the butter or margarine for the crumble in a small saucepan, add the sunflower seeds and fry very gently for a few minutes.

4. Meanwhile, mix together the other ingredients in a large bowl, rubbing in the sugar with the fingers if lumpy.

5. Pour the butter and sunflower seeds into this mixture and combine to form a loose crumble.

6. Place the fruit in a large, shallow oven-proof dish and sprinkle the crumble topping over.

7. Bake in an oven preheated to 180°C/350°F/Gas Mark 4, for about 40 minutes or until the top is golden and crisp.

TIME: Preparation takes about 20 minutes, cooking takes 50 minutes.

VARIATION: If cranberries are unavailable, substitute raspberries or redcurrants and adjust the sweetness accordingly.

SPONGE PUDDINGS WITH BLUEBERRY SAUCE

Steamed-sponge forms the basis of this deliciously different pudding. Serve with a custard sauce.

SERVES 4

175g/6oz plain flour
3 tbsps caster sugar
1 tbsp baking powder
2 eggs
15g/½oz butter, melted
Scant 120ml/4 fl oz milk
1 tbsp sweet sherry
60ml/4 tbsps blueberry jam

1. Sift together the flour, sugar and baking powder.

2. Stir in the eggs and the melted butter using a wire whisk, then gradually add the milk, mixing well after each addition to obtain a smooth paste.

3. Grease four ramekins with a little more butter and divide the mixture evenly between them. Place in a steamer over a pan of boiling water, and cover with a lid. Cook for 20 minutes or until a skewer inserted into the centre of the sponges comes out clean.

4. Add the sherry to the jam and stir well to obtain a sauce.

5. Turn the sponges out of the ramekins as soon as they are cooked, slice them and serve with the jam sauce.

TIME: Preparation takes about 20 minutes and cooking also takes about 20 minutes.

VARIATION: Use whatever jam you like.

APPLE PUDDING

This pudding makes a quick and easy dessert.

SERVES 4-6

6 eating apples
2 eggs
225ml/8 fl oz milk
225g/8oz sugar
30g/1oz butter
2 tsps baking powder
Pinch salt

1. Peel and slice the apples and layer into a lightly greased baking dish.

2. Beat the eggs in a bowl. Gradually beat in first the milk and then the sugar. Melt the butter, and stir it into the egg mixture with the baking powder and the salt.

3. Pour the egg custard over the apples, and bake in an oven preheated to 180°C/350°F/Gas Mark 4, for about 30 minutes, or until the topping mixture has set and is lightly browned.

TIME: Preparation takes 15 minutes and cooking takes 30 minutes.

VARIATION: Try using other fruit such as plums, cherries or peaches.

DE-LUXE BREAD AND BUTTER PUDDING

Serve just as it is, hot from the oven.

SERVES 4

4 thin slices wholemeal bread
A little butter
Raspberry jam
2 eggs, beaten
420ml/¾ pint milk, warmed
2 tbsps single cream
3 tbsps light muscovado sugar
1 tsp vanilla essence
2 tbsps sultanas, soaked in water for 1 hour, drained
1 tbsp dates, chopped
Grated nutmeg

1. Remove the crusts from the bread.

2. Sandwich the bread with the butter and jam and cut into small triangles.

3. Beat the eggs until foamy.

4. Add the warmed milk, cream, sugar and vanilla

5. Stir together well, making sure that the sugar has dissolved.

6. Arrange the bread triangles in a lightly buttered ovenproof dish so that they overlap and stand up slightly.

7. Scatter the dried fruits over the top.

8. Pour the egg, cream and milk mixture into the dish, ensuring that the bread triangles are saturated.

9. Grate a little nutmeg over the pudding and bake in an oven preheated to 200°C/400°F/Gas Mark 6 for about 30 minutes.

TIME: Preparation takes 10 minutes, cooking takes 30 minutes.

VARIATION: Other flavoured jams may be used instead of raspberry jam.

CLAFOUTIS

*Clafoutis was baked at harvest time in central France to satisfy appetites
sharpened by a hard day's work in the fields.*

SERVES 4

38g/5 tbsps plain flour

2 tbsps desiccated coconut

3 tbsps sugar

5 eggs

225ml/8 fl oz milk

12-16 canned cherries

1. Mix the flour, coconut and sugar together in a bowl and beat in the eggs. Add the milk a little at a time, beating well after each addition.

2. Butter one large or four small pie dishes.

3. Pour in the clafoutis batter, filling the tins no more than three-quarters full.

4. Dot the cherries evenly over the mixture.

5. Bake in an oven preheated to 180°C/350°F/Gas Mark 4, for about 25 minutes.

6. Allow to cool before serving. The clafoutis will sink as it cools.

TIME: Preparation takes about 15 minutes and cooking takes about 25 minutes.

SERVING IDEA: Serve with a little of the cherry syrup from the can.

VARIATION: Different kinds of fresh or canned fruit can be used; adjust the quantity of sugar accordingly.

RICE MERINGUE

For convenience the rice pudding and apple purée can be made in advance and assembled just before cooking the meringue.

SERVES 4

30g/1oz short grain pudding rice
570ml/1 pint milk
Few drops almond essence
75g/5 tbsps soft brown sugar
A little butter
2 large dessert apples
2 tbsps raspberry jam
2 egg whites

---

1. Wash the rice and put into a shallow, buttered ovenproof dish.

2. Add the milk, almond essence and 2 tbsps of the sugar.

3. Dot with a little butter and bake in an oven preheated to 160°C/325°F/Gas Mark 3, for 2½-3 hours, stirring two or three times during cooking.

4. Meanwhile, peel and core the apples. Slice finely and put into a saucepan with 1 tbsp of water.

5. Cook for 5-10 minutes or until softened, adding a little of the remaining sugar to sweeten. Blend in a food processor or liquidiser until puréed.

6. Cover the rice pudding with the raspberry jam, and spread the apple puree over the top.

7. Grind the remaining sugar finely and beat the egg whites until they are very stiff.

8. Fold the sugar into the egg whites and cover the pudding with the meringue mixture.

9. Using the back of a tablespoon, pull the meringue into peaks.

10. Return to the oven and bake for a further 20-30 minutes until heated through and golden on top. Serve immediately.

TIME: Preparation takes 20 minutes, overall cooking takes 3-3½ hours.

VARIATION: Make in individual ovenproof dishes.

Index